echoes

of the

heart

Musings, Poetries, Perspectives

By Shraddha Jain Magar

INDIA · SINGAPORE · MALAYSIA

ISBN 979-8-89026-453-4

Cover and Book Design: Amit Magar

To Dad

Thank you for connecting me to the beautiful world of words, which leads me to myself, and keeps me connected to you.

Love you, forever, and beyond.

I believe in perspectives. And that, they can change everything. The words on these pages depend on your perspective, and not on titles to give them meaning.

This book is not tied in titles or order, pick and read any page, as you wish.

Also, I believe in respecting love of every kind. So don't be surprised reading a he/ she/ they :)

Why a book?

There are many beautiful things around
us, which we have access to.
But every now and then, we need some-
thing of our very own. And when it
comes to words, a book you own, gives
you that feeling, like the words inside it
are your own - in reading, in immersing,
in relating, in believing, in revisiting;
something 'having access to' cannot
match.

Take a book, make the words your own.

I see a street light through my window

that keeps flickering,

a few days back it used to stay still

for a few moments at least

but now it has no rest

I wonder,

if it's a window or a mirror

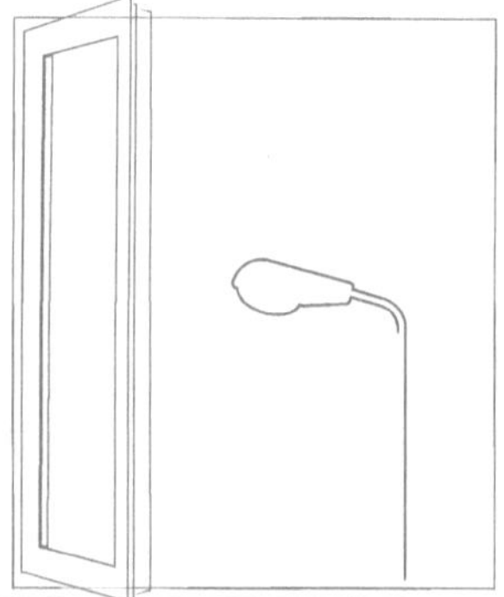

I miss love

of the kind that got intimate with the eyes

where how you held hands unfolded your feelings

where what you felt and did, overtook what you said

the kind where logics were twisted, but love was not

the kind that had different shades of fear

and fearlessness

the kind where you loved the feeling of being in love,

and yet the love for your love exceeded it

a love where nothing else mattered

yes, I miss love, that love...

Freedom

it gives me knots in my hair

yet I'd rather not tie them up

it gives me a lens of a different world

whose doors open inwards

it's fragile, it's vulnerable,

it's powerful, it's explosive

it gives me the wings

and, it gives me the weight

Do you ever feel like

travelling those roads again

where our thoughts met

and nor words mattered, nor ways

when our hands got locked

to unlock so many unknown emotions

and rewrote new languages of conversation

when our ideas and ideologies,

however different, somehow found new grounds

for agreement, and even enhancement

often I feel

I'm stuck there in time

and those moments engulf me entirely

fresh, as if, it was yesterday

Does that happen to you?

Often? Or sometimes? Or rarely at least?

Or ever?

Lying in my bed

I'm looking at the stars of radium

shining on the ceiling

something I wanted

something I really love

something I waited for

and I wonder

why the light of my phone

is overpowering everything I feel

and by the time I finish this line

and go back to my stars

they won't be as bright...

Now I get it

what happens when

love isn't nurtured

I'm waiting to feel your fragrance

as if my breath depends on it

I see the colour of the day change

and quieten my heart that's longing

to bask in the sunshine while it lasts

I remind it of all the unimportant items

on my to-do list

to-do today lists

to-do without fail lists

of the ifs and buts

of the fears,

and of freedom-that's-a-myth

of the tasks-at-hand, and not the ones in

the heart

of all the things that need to be done

before something else is done,

of the traffic in my mind

that I naively think will get cleared with

the tick marks,

cont...

of the longing and the sadness that I

think need to be ignored,

of every emotion that I bury in

between the lines of my lists

and the moments I bury between

meetings...

In the meanwhile, the sunshine is

disappearing

the natural light is going out

before the stars come out...

And I wonder looking at one

is this what I will keep doing

till I become a star myself?

'**E**verything' and 'nothing'

they may be opposites

but rarely are opposites so close to each other

shift a gear and see how

once what was everything

crumbles into nothing

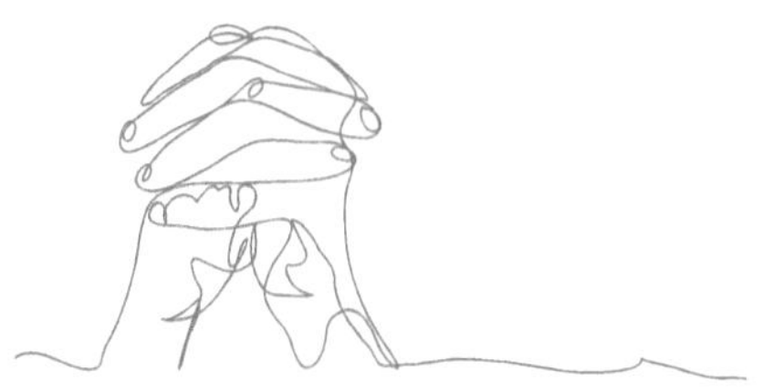

You showed me all your sacred places
and I showed you mine
and yet it couldn't save the us
we so passionately built,
nurtured and prayed for

I teach her words

she teaches me meanings

I teach her relationships

she teaches me how to keep them

I teach her action

she shows me reflection

I teach her love

she becomes its tangible form

I belong to many groups

where there's no one but me

no, actually I'm not alone

I stay there with your absence

because you were here

your fingers had left me some warmth

your bated breath had waited for me

your eyes had searched for my love

your words were here in place of this silence

your conversations had filled up everything around

your voice lit up the sky straight through WhatsApp

your smile poured life into the lifeless

your energy made the world roll faster

your questions shook my conscience

your love travelled to the deepest corner of my heart

and then

and then you

left

It feels like

a part of my heart

is walking out on me

it feels like

I'm moving from one side of darkness

to the other

it feels like

the same sadness

is waiting to engulf me

it feels like

it hurts physically

to hurt so much

it feels like

it doesn't feel like me

yet again

I keep looking at the Bougainvillea

and wonder

what went wrong

why didn't it grow

the way it almost always does

I watered the plant

I spoke to it dearly

I planted it myself

in a bigger pot than the usual

so that it has enough space to grow

I gave it some fertilizer, care and love

yet it didn't

And it keeps reminding me

of no matter what I did

I was never enough

I'm tired of growing up

tired of the responsibilities and realities that

come with age

I miss being a kid that said I want this

without having to explain why

without evaluating if I had enough money to

have it

without thinking if I deserve it

without wondering if someone needs it more,

or wants it more...

I'm tired of seeing my parents age

and wishing that I don't want to

and yet knowing

that we all are okay with the pain

as long as we keep on living

I'm surprised that the age difference

between my older and younger siblings,

is now just at a number

that's significant only in memories

I'm tired of the daily negotiations of living

while buying a car, or a house, or a pet,

or a flower for someone you love

cont...

and I'm amazed at the joy it gives us for getting
the best price
as if we have forgotten what it meant to have
negotiated on our dreams!

Isn't it surprising how lust overtakes love
love looses its charm
money becomes everything
and just proving that 'I'm someone' overtakes
everything else?!

I'm devastated in knowing that life goes on
and we come to accept it all
that a heartbreak is actually not the end of the
world
that friendships change and evolve and
silences of misunderstandings brew
and that you're made to, and are able to, with-
stand far more than that...

Oh what I wouldn't give to just go back to only
wanting the wind in my face without the need
of wheels, coz' I had my own speed and the
engine of my own heart!

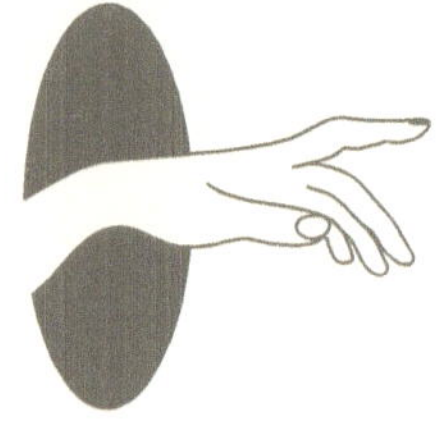 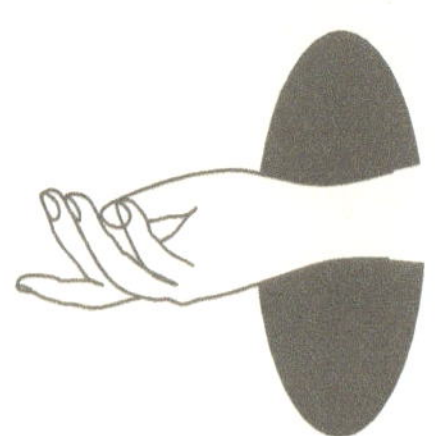

You are everywhere

like in the song I hum

that suddenly starts playing somewhere as if

the universe is, once again telling me

that we're connected...

Are you listening too?

These blank spaces that we find

between the pressure of too many responsibilities

between two nothings

between a few too many things

between seeing one post to another

between scrolling left and right

is the space we're trying to fill,

and fight

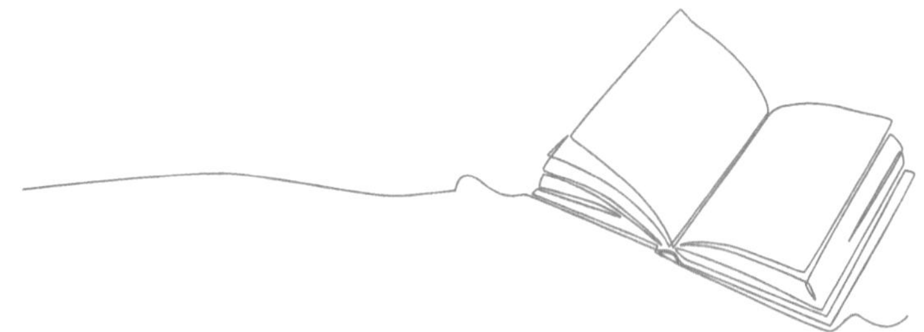

What an emptiness

to fight,

to fill,

to fuel,

to fidget,

to follow,

to fully realize

I don't know what to do with all the love I have

in my heart

maybe it's not enough to make someone feel com-

pletely loved

maybe it's not enough for loyalty

maybe it's not one that lasts a lifetime

maybe it's just for those who are sufficiently away

maybe it's for strangers who want me and

not for those who have accepted me

not for those who see the cracks but for those who

don't know where the cracks are

maybe it's stifled under expectations, but

it still breathes

what do I do with those half breaths

those incomplete dreams I'm closer to than

the fulfilled ones

what do I do with this love in my heart?

As sounds set

loneliness dawns

Let's keep the complexities of love away

I just need the comfort of your kindness

your warmth, your friendship

I don't want to embark on a way

where we may have to choose

anything otherwise

and love, often love is what takes us there

I sit without you

looking at the stars

the difference

is the one between being alive and

just being

the difference

is in holding your hands to

holding my tears back

the difference

is in the cool breeze getting warmer to

the cool breeze getting harsher

the difference

is between us to now, you and me

In the stillness of the night

lying thoughtless

the moon is beautiful but quiet

the sky has its shades but it doesn't talk

to me

the crickets are doing their best

to break the silence

but they don't know the language

in which

silences are broken for us

it's not the language of words

it's the language of love

I saw that place the second time today

and I started noticing many little things

that escaped my eye when I was wearing

the lens of new

the first time, I only noticed a few...

a quiet guitar, so many books ruffled

through, closely interacted with,

subtly outlining a characteristic...

the minimalism, the excessive that never

made place, the light scent - light on its

feet for making its presence felt without its

clutches...

but I didn't notice what I observe now

a little paper folded neatly to keep the

table from moving, a corner of a room

with a fresh web,

cont...

the little lines on the curtains, the books

out of alignment but in tune with the

characteristics, the number of chairs

enough for a group, the guitar case not

gathering dust...

and most of all,

a calming voice that echoes in my mind,

and a smile wrinkled with compassion at

the edges and the effect, as if it's all

absorbed by the walls, the rug, the books,

the lamps, the candle, the glasses, the

chairs and the air that moves here...

each of them making an effort to tell me

how much more there is to know

how many details we fail to see while they

lie in front of us

how the little signs of effort are

everywhere

and that the design of the universe is

so beautiful, only if we see it

I'd filled some bottles with our memories

some with the fragrance of your skin

some with the fragrance of your free hair

some bottles with the fragrance of frangipani

with the subtleties and beauty of our conversations

and the tiredness after our long walks

that paused right below the frangipani tree

I also have some empty bottles that have us

all over them

sometimes I literally hear the sound of our laughter

coming straight out of them

and taste the salt of our tears from the same bottles

they've held on the nights we escaped out to be free

without an expiry date

some bottles have fragrances we shared as one and

some have that of our individuality

these bottles are now my window to our world

a world of our memories

coz' that's all I am left with...

And then there are people who don't even

need to see you

to know that something is wrong

and then there are those who see you and

still wouldn't know...

yet we are chasing the latter

Alone, aren't we?

Even in togetherness

even in loneliness

maybe that's exactly

how it's supposed to be

maybe that's exactly

what the ultimate truth is -

you and your mirror

I feel like I've broken a sacred place...

is there any forgiveness?

A post

a story

a blank window

a no-new-message

a string of new msgs

a no-new-mail

to too many mails to check

a busy looking day

a busy looking week

a silent weekend

a bold lipstick

a matching earring

a beautiful dress

a tick mark on the to-do

are all quiet misleads on feelings

what you choose to read

is what you choose to read

Words, the friends

words, the traps

words, the carriers

words, the burdens

words, the flags

words, the cheats

words, the loyalists

words, the crooks

words, the saviours

words, the solace

words, the thorns

words, the completeness

words, always incomplete

And then

what you counted on the most, is taken away,

without you knowing why

what you flaunted to the world for acceptance

suddenly became judgmental

what you thought was perfect

started to show the cracks

what you thought was an anchor

went away floating... far far away

and then you wonder

was that a dream?

or is this a dream?

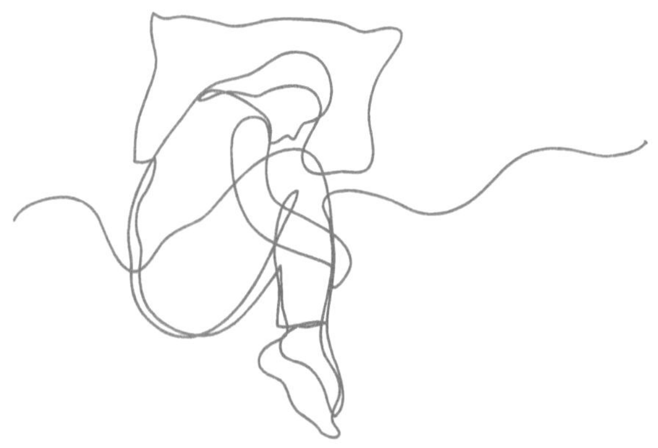

These moments of quiet

are scary and dear at the same time

the journey of finding myself

and the fear of what will I find

Consumed by

the desire

to be held close

by another shape

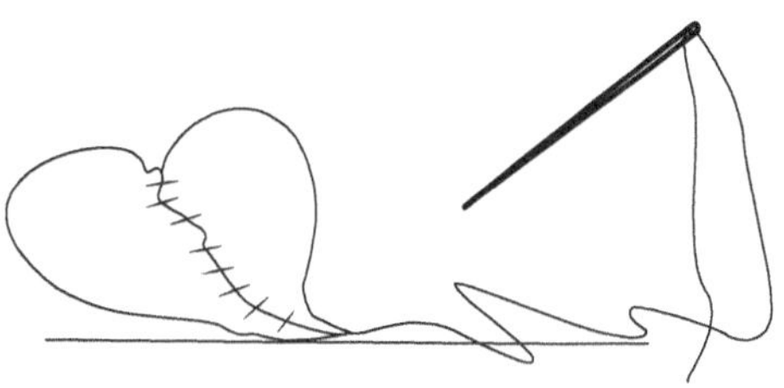

How many heart aches

can a heart bear?

Doesn't it sometimes seem easier to love

things than people?

They don't question, they don't assume,

they don't react

they don't complain "you're not the same

anymore!"

their expectations are always limited to your

own imagination

and you can decide

how they feel about you...

Is that why we're running after things, rather

than people?

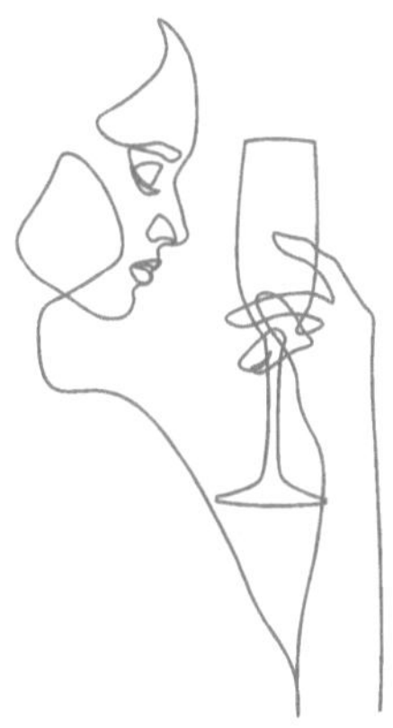

Sunday is a mix feeling cocktail

a little sweet

a little bitter

a little like a breakup love letter

they say they still love you

but they can't be with you forever

maybe love means to be like a Sunday

you know it'll come

but you also know it'll go

Do relationships have a shelf life?

No not in the sense of a timeline

in the sense of subject to...

subject to one being patient

subject to one being selfless

subject to one not putting up their own thoughts

subject to one listening

subject to one being able to provide

or subject to how many scars one has on them

subject to how much one can absorb

or how much one can let go

subject to how much someone can take one for

granted, or exactly the opposite

subject to how selfish one is

subject to how crazy one is

subject to being oneself completely

and once this subject is dropped

the relationship goes puff

like a bomb that didn't make a sound

but has still managed to destroy everything,

absolutely everything

Sometimes getting too close

suffocates

Yes you miss them

the way they made you smile

the way they just got you

the way they uncovered the deepest side of

you

the manner in which they held your hand

the passion with which they kissed you

how they made your heartbeat dance

the rhythm with which you could flow with

them

how they tried to correct everything around

you

how they gave themselves to mend you

how they protected you, sometimes even

from yourself

how they lit up your eyes like you had

sunshine of your own

how they came into your lives when you

really needed them

how they changed you

how they taught you

how they learned from you

how they fought with you

cont...

how you felt it was something that would last

forever

something you wanted too

and yet it didn't

and yet you chose to not go back

and yet you couldn't overcome the damage of

harsh words

and couldn't make sense of your feelings, until

they were way out of hand

and the fear of losing actually made you lose

each other

yes, we miss them

yes, it's complicated

Always and never

maybe two extremes,

but for me, they have one thing in common

they say never say never

I say, never say always

My eyes are so heavy

my mind is on a marathon

a half baked presentation prep

a meaningless compliment

an incomplete conversation with a friend

that word I could have used instead of another

that hug I didn't give my brother

the words that could calm someone

my mind on a marathon

of running away from every thought

that matters

of running away from answers

that will lead to more questions

of running away from reasons why my eyes

are so heavy in the first place

of running away from myself

of letting me add another brick to

curb my feelings

and finding words and poetry to run

further away

my mind, on a marathon...

I watch the sunshine from my room

imagining how lovely the little leaves

are feeling in its light

I feel the urge to take the step I've always longed

to but never have taken

coz' there's always something else to do

some guilt to address

some responsibility to fulfill

reminding myself of another unkept promise

something that will weigh nothing as opposed to

my smile in that sunshine

and knowing it all

in the fraction of a second

I let another day of sunlight go

Some joy that flies away

and sadness that stays

some wounds that we forgot about, still pain

some pain we forgot, that changed us

some rough sketches of wishes

some rare moments of truth

some beautiful sunrays through the trees

some butterflies of curiosity

some touches of something more

some touches of something less

some attractions, some attachments

some tugs of war of attention

some dark desires

sometimes the light of compassion

some fake smiles

some sparkles in the eyes

a little something of so many things

a little too much of too many things

oh life, how many shades do you exactly have?

It's new to be with you

I said to the mirror

the mirror agreed, saying

how busy have you been

looking for yourself

in all the wrong places

Monuments that stand

the test of time and hardships

yet stand tall in all their glory

are far more celebrated

than the perfect ones...

Isn't it time we celebrate

ourselves just the same?

You can fill your time with things to do
but not the holes in your heart

What is the measure of success

the sq.ft. of your house

the leg room of your car

or the size of the diamond on your ring

is it the number of people waiting

to meet you everyday

or the size of the number in your bank account

what is the measure of success

or is it the width of your smile

and the number of times it reaches your eyes

is it the peace your voice gives to someone

is it the number of hearts you've comforted

and how many burdens you've tried to lighten

or is it the optimism of life that fills you up

success is many things

let's not confuse it, with just money

A few drops of sunshine

I've stored in a bottle you gave me

I've also stored some fragrance

in some of my breaths

The light of darkness

like a stroke of compassion in a prisoner

or a rebel streak in a commoner

like finding a reason to smile

even amidst a hurricane

like a good old friend who accepted you

in all your darkness

like the comfort of the unknown

like being found in spite of still being lost

like being held when you feel like

you don't deserve it

like finding butterflies amidst traffic jams

like the love in your heart for someone

who broke it

Sunshine

where are you

it's just raining clouds

it's just raining storms

where's the hand that held mine

to make sunshine happen

and sometimes, even rainbows

I called you

and you came

I kept looking at the window

and you showed up

you waited there for a minute or two

I looked at you

with eyes so full

with heartbeats racing

with my heart aching at the distance

but my lips that couldn't grasp anything more

than the fact that you'd come

I held your hands

I touched your cheeks

I gave you a hug that broke me and built me at the
same time

my eyes couldn't let go off your eyes

together they said a prayer

and that moment gave me

everything I've ached for and everything I'll ache for

I don't know for how long...

She comes to meet me every day

appearing online just when I open her

chat window

and we both talk in silence

so much to say, so much to hear

but no words to exchange

They come to me via the sound waves of
the world...
when the azaan brings the texture of their
hands into mine

they come to meet me in the breeze that stays
somewhere close, no matter the season

they stay with me through my prayers
they didn't just give me faith back when I shut
my eyes
they gave me a world I could trust with my
eyes open

they live inside me like distance is a myth
and we chose it coz' we are the gift of magi

Some days, the days when I've laughed a little

days that I've tried to live a little

come back and haunt me with your absence

My heart feels so sad so often

but I often forget the reason

I have now started asking it

what's your excuse today?!

Don't you sometimes think

that closeness has elasticity

no matter how close you are

it always has bandwidth for more

and no matter how close you are

it can sometimes just not accommodate

Seeing dad in the hospital

I can't stop thinking about love and life

and everything that lies in between

and even after

I wonder if love stays

even after we travel to the other side

and as I type other side

my thoughts wander

as my heart leaps and weeps

that you're not on my side

even on earth

In this world of love and lovers

can't I find one friend who's a friend

who doesn't have questions

who doesn't have expectations

who doesn't want me to do something first

who can read what I'm feeling

who can make me talk

who can comfort me while I'm comforting others

who can talk to me and who I can talk to

who answers silences

no I don't want to be a radio

I don't want just a listener

I want someone who listens but also asks

helps me find answers

helps me read my feelings

even better, myself

that's all that I need for now

is anyone, absolutely anyone, all those

who just love me included...

is anyone listening?

It hurts to think

hurts like my heart is tearing apart

hurts to have had you

and lost you again

hurts to have had you

and hurt you again

hurts to have no answers

to any questions again

hurts to be myself

all over again

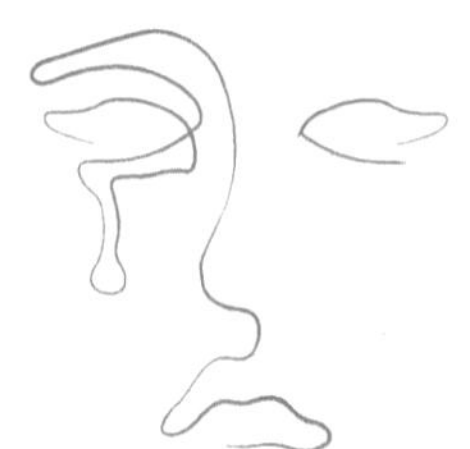

Hope

running helter-skelter

in the corridors of an ICU

hope

that dies in

a lover's eyes

hope

that helps you drag your feet

and your breath

on the toughest days

hope

that you come to hate on days

for all the dreams it gave you

and they broke

and the corners of these

pierce deeper every time

hope

that you still can't let go of

sometimes like a toxic relationship

sometimes like warmth for your cold feet

sometimes like the only thread you can count on

like a tear that trickles down

the corner of your lover's eye

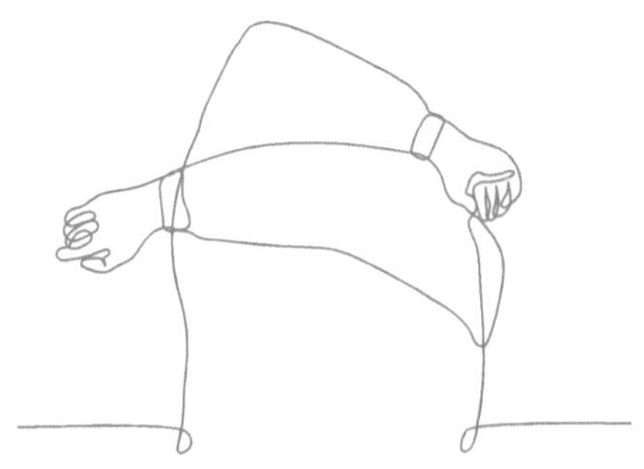

The thing with honesty
is that it often pierces,
the thing with me is
I avoid anything that does

when you face confrontation
it causes discomfort
and I like comfort
in the face of anything

balance is what makes everyone happy
but what it really does is
makes you happy
coz' you're not an eye sore anymore

balance, comfort, softness
are walls behind which we hide
to save face, to save our perception
to save ourselves from our real selves

Not today

i tell my inferiority complex

today i need to go

to meet that side of me

that I've waited for all my life

not today

Sometimes seeing a bit

of the vast sky

is all you need

to feel

that life's worth it all

When they say strong

I wonder if they're mistaking it for

stone

when they say 'the sane one'

I wonder why do I hide my insanity

when they choose me

I know they don't know who I am

It's weird

how every time anyone chooses me

and every time they don't

I feel the same ache

That moment

when you pause Netflix

when you stop the auto mode of life

and ask yourself

what is it that you're feeling

that moment is the blessing we need

Let's talk anything

but please don't say the 3 words

let's talk the weather, the time,

the season

let's talk about the pets, and let's talk

about the books

the ones to keep and the ones to let go

the ones to hold on to with dear heart

let's talk about yesterday and let's talk

about tomorrow

let's talk about regrets and let's talk

about dreams

let's talk about work and let's talk about

words

let's talk about love and poetry and

philosophy and life

let's talk about nature's beauty and about

art

and their irreplaceability

cont...

let's talk places to go

let's talk about broken dreams

let's talk about shadows and lights

and darkness and character

let's talk about loyalty and infidelity

let's talk till the sun comes up

but don't just say the 3 dreaded words

"how are you?"

don't stump me

don't leave me wordless

don't salt my wounds

don't make me go there

I'm putting up a face

I'm killing time everyday

so much that on a busy day

I'd forget myself

I'd laugh and I'd bubble away

until someone asks

"how are you, today?"

The walk alone

one where the stars and moon are not

company

they're loneliness

where the silence isn't beautiful

it stings

where the weight of wishes is also as heavy

as the weight of expectations

where the sunshine

always comes with sunburns

where you being your own company

is not welcome but inevitable

the walk alone

in all its darkness

is still honest

is still an opening

to a road

that leads to yourself

Of all the relationships we see around us

how many would be still intact
if we broke the mould of society?

how many would still exist
if we withdrew transaction?

how many would still continue
if we removed children from the equation?

how many would still go on
if we freed people from self-reflection?

and after all these filters are applied
the ones that remain

how much do we do for those relationships
other than write a few lines
or shed a few tears?

I comb my hair these days

they aren't free, tangled, messy anymore

I don't think I like this better

but it sure hurts lesser

I don't know how many sunsets I've missed
to some ridiculous to-do lists
can't imagine the number of mornings I've missed
coz' my eyes were too tired from crying
don't have a count of how many wishes of mine
I didn't even acknowledge
just because someone, anyone had laid out theirs
and then I wonder why I don't know myself,
why don't I love myself or feel incomplete...
but now that I know better
I'm taking myself out of my own way
to make way for myself

Purpose is an illusion

moments is the reality

What do you do now

that all your little wars inside are over

that now your heart doesn't beat to the moon

now that your enthusiasm and nothingness are

interchangeable

now that your eyes just hurt, and tear up

without knowing why

now that loneliness and chaos feel the same

now that, what mattered, doesn't matter

now that every time the sunrises,

the effort is real...

now, where do you go from here?

Last month

my biggest sorrow

was a heartbreak

which suddenly seems

like the world was still intact

at least all the pieces of life

were present

they may have been helter-skelter

they may not have been exactly like I wanted

but they were there

silently breathing without sound

until one day

the breathing of one extremely important piece

stopped

and suddenly everything that felt so big

started feeling small

the pain, the suffering magnified

and the ability to do something about it - nullified

In distance I love

in closeness I repel

No February

you're not the month of love

you're not the month of flowers

you're not the month of togetherness

you're not the month of the sweet nothings

or the month of counting stars together

you're the month of ugly realities

you're the month of bare wilderness that brings

flowers only on deathbeds

you're the month of taking away

taking away not just aspirations and ambitions

but taking away dreams and hopes

you're far far away from love

the love that basks in its one sidedness

you make that love realise how incomplete it is

you tear people up with fears

cont...

and yes if you are at all about stars

it's about those that we see with tears in our eyes

the stars of loss

and the stars of incomplete wishes

the stars you keep going back to

because you miss some people so much

you're not butterflies in the stomach

you're the lump in throats that

are made by the holes that will never fill up

No february, you're not love,

you're the loss of love

Just when we expect the edges of the world to
soften coz' you just can't take it anymore,
just when we're so vulnerable that the smallest
prick can crack your soul,
just when you need that hand on your shoulder
and that warm hug and that conversation that
means something,
it all goes amiss... puff!
just when you need Him to listen to you so badly,
He shows you the mirror of karma!

They leave us and go

and we,

try collecting all our pieces

scattered across memories...

But no matter how many we collect,

can we ever be the same again?

I see ants, many ants

trying with all their strength

to pick up one grain

they're not alone

they're together

trying to carry a weight

that would be too heavy for one

and here I am

carrying the grain of my grief

all alone

wondering where is my together

Driving, I saw a car right ahead of me

with a big dent on its booty

a mark that the owner may not be looking at everyday

but it must've really pained her at the time it happened

or that scratch that is far more subtle now

must've bothered her for days

or that side mirror that has changed form

than what it originally was

but now she's got used to this new form

and wonder took me by storm...

isn't that relationship with her car

is how our relationship is with ourselves

we bear scratches of judgments

we withstand the pain of going through separations

we get dents with broken relationships

we change form when we lose someone

and yet we accept ourselves in a new form so often

and yet we keep driving

we brave through the roads

like everything is alright

we smile and we carry on

looking behind sometimes

and looking ahead most times

How long have I waited for you,

and knowing

how short lived your stay is going to be

still doesn't make my spirit frown

as the moment fills me with so much joy

the thought of tomorrow has no window

I come to see you everyday

I admire you right below the scorching sun

I see you as the day changes into night

your beauty only multiplying

everyday up and down this lane I go

everyday going wherever you go

wherever you grow

admiring every detail of your shower

I don't know what looking at you does to me

I just know I'm in a happy trance

and I will bask in its glory

cont...

while it lasts

until summer comes again

and fills up with 'Golden Showers' again

and I wonder what will I do until you're back

and I smile at the simplicity of the answer

I'll wait

I'll wait for you golden flowers

just like I wait every season, every year

I'll wait for you all over again

and I'll come to meet you at all the same places again

and find you in new corners of the city

creating new places for us to create memories

just you and me

Is emptiness real?

or is it a feeling you draw onto yourself

is it something that everyone feels

maybe in different degrees of severity

maybe in different forms

like questions, like gaps,

maybe even in eloquence?

does this longing, which has no answer

as to what it is for, qualify as longing?

does it multiply this emptiness?

It's often cold outside

or then its scorching hot

where is the warmth I wonder

Some grief is so personal

that no matter how much you share it

no matter how much you talk about it

no matter how much you cry on someone's shoulder

it's still your own

just your own

The sound of the azaan

muffled with the breeze

the half setting sun

scattered over the evening

the shades of the sky

soaked in your memory

the sound of chaos

making appeals of peace

for a place in my heart, forever

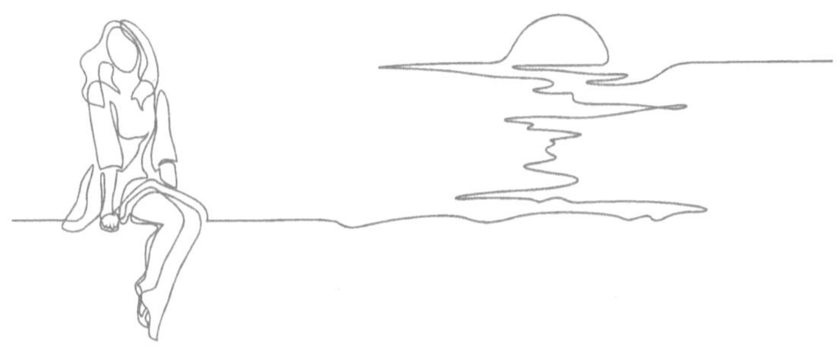

I didn't choose earrings for myself today

and surprisingly

the ones that I always look at,

the ones I hold, touch and drift into memories

the ones I never pick

coz' they make me feel so close to you

and remind me of the unbearable pain

of being away from you...

those were the ones picked for me

by someone else

and I don't know why

I just decided to flow with the pain today

I just decided to feel your love again today

I just decided to let that hole in my heart remain

Their traces are all over me

in those half taken breaths, that refuse to

complete now

in all those trails I don't walk and just lie in

my bed instead

on the pillows that get wet

every now and then

where your fragrance used to wander

in those stars that still twinkle

but bring me the flip side

in the mirror that wears a smile

but in the eyes that don't

I don't want to be seen today

I want to get camouflaged into my surroundings

I want to get lost in all that's unimportant

I don't want any attention

any empathy, any words, any touch

I just want silence and non-existence

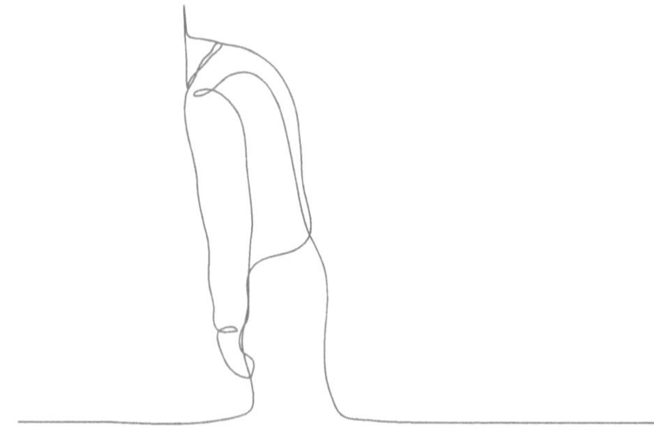

Sometimes noise is peace
remember... every trip in school?
sometimes chaos is solace
an excuse for the mind to stop thinking
and sometimes you don't want what you seek
coz' the thrill of the chase is beautiful

What kind of love did you want when

you were younger

and then when you were a little older

than that

what kind of love would you want

today

and a few years from now?

Love changes...

the definition of love,

the expectations from love,

and also the love you're capable of...

I lost a poetry to my tired eyes

and it feels like sand slipping off,

my feet losing earth

and time running out on me, just like my wishes are

and like every time my therapist calls me to healing,

I'm busy being hurt

and like the fireflies I've never seen,

those words will never come to life

in the raw and beautiful and imperfect form

they were forming in my heart

Have you ever experienced

the pain of sheer existence

of knowing that being there

is not making any difference...

when the leaves moving to the breeze

seem to hold a bigger purpose than you

when you see the light the fireflies hold

and look at the dark side of you

you who can talk and do

you who can mend and make

you who can think and move

you who is so bound by so much

you who could be so free

From here to somewhere else

from head to heart

from heart to soul

from soul to distance

from distance to apart

from apart to hurt

from hurt to pain

from pain to numbness

from numbness to tears

from tears to nowhere

from nowhere to smiles

from smiles to somewhere else

from somewhere else

to somewhere else

the story of moving on

never stops

Windows everywhere

in between moving from one screen to another

in between one household chore to another

in between bills

and in between responsibilities

in between calls

and in between meals

in between the skewed work life balance

in between the traffic jams, of the roads, and

the heart

in between the blessings and curses of luxuries

in between the needs and wants

in between the shoulds and should nots

in between the string of complaints

in between the crowd of ifs and buts

in between the pulls and pushes of life

in between it all

there are windows

windows of moments

to look into our soul

cont...

windows of smiles of self love

windows of pop colours in the sky

windows of the leaves moving to the breeze

windows of some long lost conversations

windows of beautiful flowers by the road side

windows of kids in the rain

windows of observing a caterpillar cross

windows of remembering someone without a purpose

windows of a prayer for someone not dear to you

windows of deeper meanings

windows of smelling a book

windows of shutting your eyes

windows of connections

windows of a free breath

how many windows do you open everyday?

Do you sometimes just crave the feeling

of falling in love?

of being wrapped around someone's little finger

of that anxious wait where every minute feels like

slow poison

of feeling the butterflies reach from your stomach

to your eyes at the brush of a touch

when the blood rush doesn't just blush your cheeks

but runs through your core

when you could just keep looking at that person

without a blink, finding every nuance adorable

when your conversations with them continue

even when they're not around

moments when you could get high

on the laughter you share

cont...

when every little emotion is so heightened,

it's like a view from the sky

like being amidst those clouds,

doesn't it just make you feel so alive

as if it's an addiction

as if it's the only reason for our existence

and maybe it is...

until it grows, stales or fades

and until we long for that feeling

all over again...

does it happen with you?

When I look into the mirror

I look so beautiful

there's a sheen on my skin

and a spark in my eyes

as I move out

as I interact with the world

as I start comparing

I start hampering

I start tampering

I begin to find fault with my strengths

I begin to widen my gaps

I begin to question my answers

I let the dust of it all

settle on my shine

until I start looking dull to myself

until I start making the mirror lie to me

and suddenly

my mirror decided to speak to me this morning

it showed me how my cracks made me real

it asked me about this blanket of passion I had that's

now just a streak

it asked me who was killing what made me, me

and could it ever be anyone else?

and if it couldn't be anyone else, who could fix it?

I used to see my mom

trying to sleep on the floor of our big living room

I remember her eyes

as if they were searching for something

I guess

as much as she liked the big living room

she missed the simple joys

which she tried to find by lying on the floor

but which didn't find their way to her eyelids

to give her some peaceful sleep

often I would try sleeping next to her

thanks to the innocence of childhood

and the blessing of having mom next to me

I'd sleep, sharing her cushion...

and ever since,

her eyes make me question

where does my happiness lie?

does it reach my eyelids when I'm trying to sleep?

All I want to do is run away

from every thing, from every something

from the search that I don't even understand is what

exactly for

from the emptiness that I can't shake off

from everything I know to be true

from everything I know to be is false

from this familiarity and from this love for it

from these expectations and how they drown me

from this constant ask from myself for something more,

something different

from this dependency on others for feeling complete

from this non-dependency

that then turns into hollowness

from these shadows of distance and closeness

from these clutches of attention that tear through my

skin

and most of all this love that comes at odd times, often

unasked for

and yet eludes me forever

as I keep looking for it, staring at myself

what do I do to be free?

where do I run away?

If I ever go away

will you come looking for me?

will you miss me enough

to make a difference?

will you feel this hole in your heart

that I feel now?

Sometimes I just want to opt out

of this competition

of not having dressed well enough

not looking good enough

not knowing enough gossip

of not earning enough money

of just not being enough

it's just so tiring

sometimes I'd rather

just sit in my bubble

and just be

Like the skin has layers

I'm sure the heart has too

and every layer has emotions...

the multiple feelings

we're feeling in every moment

but the thing I often wonder about

is that why is the deepest layer of sadness

and why does it just stay

amidst all other emotions

why is it such a constant?

I read a quote that asked me,

"who were you before they broke your heart?"

and I thought,

I broke into so many pieces that I don't

remember if I collected all of myself

I wonder

how many windows pay attention

to the flickering light I see outside my window

the light on which I write so many poems

the light which I think is with me

on this journey

the light I find a lot like me

flickering

sometimes in confidence

sometimes in enthusiasm

sometimes in perseverance

sometimes in setting expectations

sometimes blinking through love

sometimes shaken through bad weather

sometimes just not as it should be

and always not as its expected to be

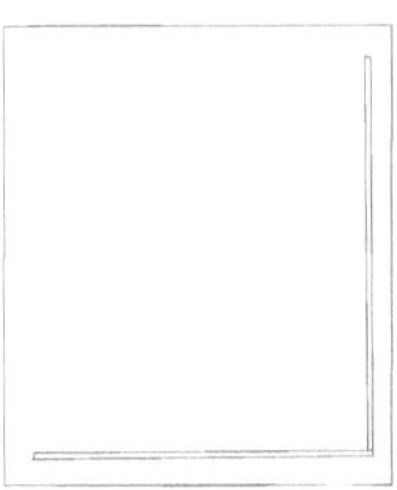
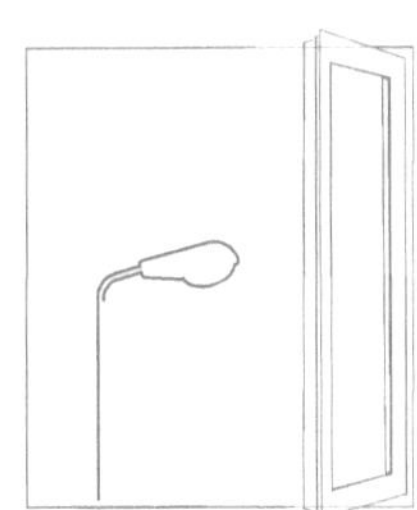

In your arms I used to embrace myself too

now, how will I do that ever again?

In a land deprived of water

where plants struggle to grow

you suddenly see a sea of Bougainvillea

of your favourite colour

a favourite you shared with your favourite person

the beauty of the contrast

and the ache of how much you miss that person

strike you in equal measure

and then the latter takes over

Through the world lens

success looks very stiff and cold

through the inward lens however

everything flows

in different directions

in different colours

not bound by any definitions

and no matter what shape, form, size it has...

this definition of success

is warm, really warm

like the love for yourself

warm like smiles and soft sunshine

and warm like life itself...

how does your success make you feel?

After light, the darkness gets unbearable

but for those who have always stayed in darkness,

darkness has it's own light

Why does it rain in summer?

is it someone we love sending these showers

from up there to cool our scorching souls?

or is it karma that comes with a mask

only to make it worse after the showers?

I'd like to believe the former

and make the most of this moment

when the breeze and the rain embrace

my spirit that was being drained by the sun...

Tgif

thank God it's Friday

thank God there's space for dreams

in between chases

thank God there are two days reserved for life

thank God we sometimes slow down

to tune our own hearts

God alone knows who told us,

it could all be done only when weeks end

and yet, thank God it's Friday!

Yes I talk to strangers these days

sometimes about my deepest feelings

I don't know why but

only that feels like I'm not betraying you

Sunsets

don't they sometimes look so beautiful

that they make you forget everything else

the sadness as much as the laughter

the wounds as much as the balms

the hurt as much as the love

just life afloat

meditating between it all...

would death also feel like that?

when the final sun sets?

What is peace?

when your mind and heart agree to disagree...

when someone puts your feelings into words...

when you accept to flow...

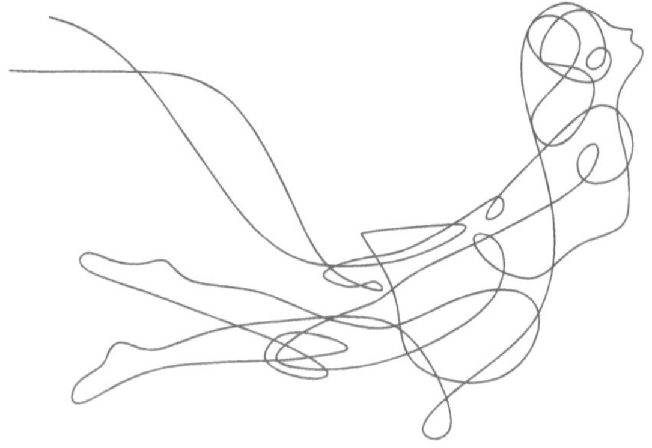

Would love to hear what you thought about this book at *shraddhaandherwords@gmail.com*

For more poetries, more books, more stories, and many more musings...

- Shraddha_and_her_words
- Shraddha_and_her_words
- Shraddha_and_her_words

A heartfelt

and humungous

thank you

to my entire family

for being

by my side, always!